Ginger

Pupil's Book 4

Allgemeine Ausgabe – Neubearbeitung
Lehrwerk für Englisch ab Klasse 3

Überarbeitet von
Kerstin Caspari-Grote, Ina Grandt,
Ulrike Kraaz, Claudia Neuber,
Christel Simon, Ines Völtz
auf der Grundlage der Ausgabe von
Birgit Hollbrügge und Ulrike Kraaz

Cornelsen

Contents

Symbols

🦔	read	💿 listen CD 1.24	🎭 act out
💬	talk		

A postcard from Ginger

  Read.

 Talk.

London
_____

Dear Captain Storm,

I'm in London. It's great.
Please come to London!
Say hello to all the children,
please.

From,
Ginger

To

Captain Storm
_____

London sights

  1 Listen.
CD 1.6

  2 Read.

 **3** Talk.

This is Big Ben.
It has got a big clock.

This is the London Eye.
You can see London
from the top.

This is Victoria Station.
It's a train station.

This is Tower Bridge.
It's over the River Thames.

This is London Zoo.
A lot of animals live here.

This is Buckingham Palace.
The Queen lives here.

Einen Hörtext verstehen, über Sehenswürdigkeiten sprechen ▶ S.89

At London Zoo

1 Talk.   2 Read.

... is climbing
... is eating
... is drinking
... is looking at
... is playing
... is sleeping
... is sitting

Look at the funny monkeys!

I'd like to see the parrots.

Here you are, a lemon ice cream.

ice

Ginger in London

Dick Whittington

 **1** Talk.    **2** Read the story.

Once upon a time there was a boy. His name was Dick Whittington.
He was very poor. He lived in a small town.

1

Where are you going?

To London. I want to be rich.

2

Good luck.

The next morning Dick was in London.
What a big city! What a big river!
What a lot of big houses! What a lot of big bridges!
But there was no gold on the streets of London.

Are you sad?

Yes, I am.

I'm tired and I'm hungry.

Come to my house. My father is rich. He has got a big house. He can give you a job.

3

4

Eine Geschichte lesen ▶ S. 104

One morning Dick put on his socks.
Oh, no! There was a hole in his
sock! He put on his shoes. There
was a hole in his shoe!

Oh, no! There's a hole in my sock!

*Rats!
Rats in the kitchen.
Rats on the table.
Rats under the chair.*

Dick was a good helper
in the kitchen.

Thank you.

*Well done, Dick.
Here's a penny.*

Now Dick had a penny. He was
happy. There was a cat in a shop.

Here's a penny.

Here's the cat.

Now Dick had a cat. He was very
happy. There was a rat under
Dick's bed …

Good cat.

I like rats!

Spotlight Landeskunde: A London museum

 **1** Read.

Madame Tussauds is a museum in London. There are famous people in the museum: pop stars, film stars, sports stars and kings and queens. The people in the museum are made of wax.

2 Talk.

> Mr Bean • Lady Gaga • Prince William • Katy Perry • David Beckham

3 Make an accordion book of famous people.
You need: a piece of paper, glue, pictures, a round split pin, some string

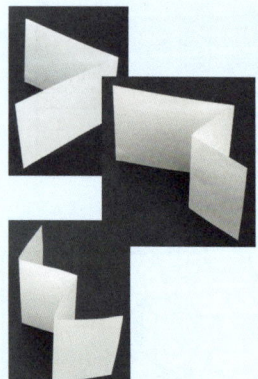

Fold the paper (like an accordion).

Write the name of the book on the cover page and illustrate it. Make a small hole and fix the split pin to the cover page.

Glue your pictures into the book.

Fix some string around the split pin, so you can close your book.

Einen Sachtext lesen, bekannte Personen vorstellen ▸ S. 107/108

An invitation from Debbie's brother

1 Read the text message.

2 Talk about the pictures.

> beach • beach ball •
> beach towel • kite • sea •
> sunglasses • sun hat •
> swimming costume/trunks

Bill

Hi Debbie,
Come to Los Angeles.
The weather is great.
It's sunny and really
warm.
See you soon!

Let's all go to the beach!

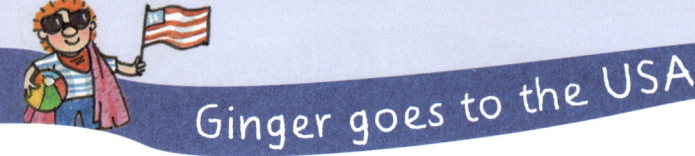

A film crew on the beach

CD 1.21
1 Listen.

2 Talk about the picture.

3 Read the speech bubbles.

Einen Hörtext verstehen, einen Dialog lesen ▸ S. 117/118

On the beach

1 Talk about the picture.

2 Read the sentences. Right or wrong?

1. There's a kite in the sea.
2. There's a beach ball on a beach towel.
3. There's a sandcastle under a blue and red kite.
4. There are seashells in the sand.
5. There are two beach balls under a basket.

3 Make more sentences.

Sports

1 Talk about the pictures.

American football • badminton • baseball • basketball • football • table tennis • volleyball

2 Talk to a partner. *Can you play baseball? – Yes, I can. / No, I can't.*

Spotlight Landeskunde: The USA

 1 Read the sentences. Match the pictures.

People from all over the world live in the USA.

> They're from Ireland:
> In March there's a big Irish parade
> in New York.
> Everybody wears green clothes.

> They're from Germany:
> In the picture you can see a
> German basketball player.

> They're from China:
> There are a lot of Chinese
> shops in American cities.

> They're from Mexico:
> You can buy Mexican food everywhere.
> Do you like Mexican food?

 2 Make a Mexican wrap.
You need: a wrap, carrots, cheese, chilli sauce, lettuce, sour cream

 **1** Put sour cream and lettuce on your wrap.

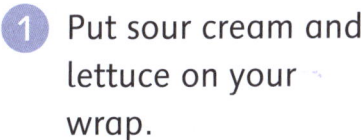 **4** Fold your wrap.

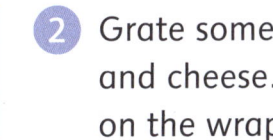 **2** Grate some carrots and cheese. Put it on the wrap.

Enjoy your Mexican wrap.

 **3** Put some chilli sauce on the wrap.

A letter for Captain Storm

1 Talk about the pictures.

2 Read the letter.

Dear Grandpa,

How are you? I'm fine.
Mum, Dad, Eric and Lizzy are
fine, too. We want to go camping
in the Rocky Mountains.
I know that you like camping.
Can you come?
Please!

Love,
Sarah

Einen Brief lesen, Bilder beschreiben ▸ S. 133

At the camping store

1 Talk about the picture.

CD 1.39 **2** Listen.

$16 $30 $19 $9 $21
$45 $85
$74 WARM SLEEPING BAG

$73 $56 $81

BIG TENT
$99
$25
$18

How much is it?

$33

$18 $13
$8
WATER BOTTLE

$7 $11
$20 SMALL POCKET KNIFE

$27

The bear and the beaver

1 Play the game.

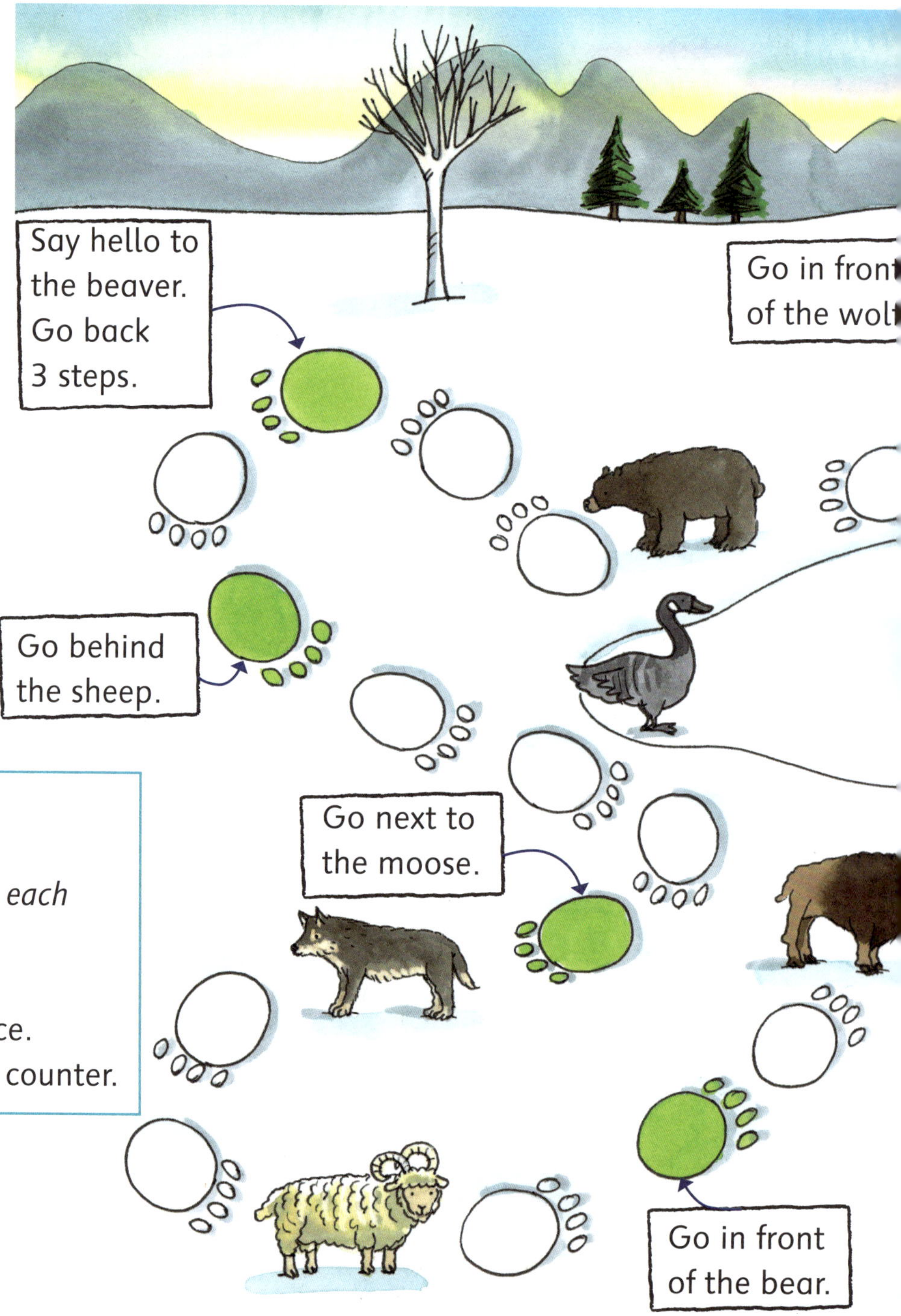

Say hello to
the beaver.
Go back
3 steps.

Go in front
of the wolf

Go behind
the sheep.

You need:
a dice
a counter for each
player

• Roll the dice.
• Move your counter.

Go next to
the moose.

Go in front
of the bear.

Ein Spiel spielen ▸ S. 147

Go behind the bear.

START

Go next to the goose.

Say hello to the beaver. Go back I step.

Go behind the buffalo.

FINISH

Spotlight Landeskunde: The Inuit in Canada

1 Talk.

2 Listen.
CD 1.45

Nunavut: Our land
(31 000 people, 85 % Inuit)
Capital: Iqaluit

Canadian money

The flag of Nunavut:
North star, Inukshuk,
yellow – soil, white – snow

In Canada, in Nunavut,
The Inuit live there,
The language is Inuktitut,
Nanuq – the polar bear.

Animals: Nanuq – polar bear

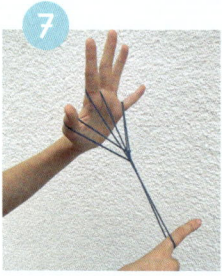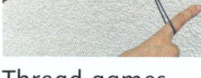

Inukshuk: Man of
stone

Inuit traditions:

Thread games

Throat singing

Transport: dog sled

3 Read.

Language: Inuktitut, English
Transport: snow mobiles, dog sleds, planes. There are no streets.
Animals: polar bear, arctic fox, seal, caribou, whale, walrus
Inuit traditions: hunting, fishing, storytelling, throat singing, thread games
Inuk / Inuit: man / men
Asujutilli: Hello! **Tavvauvutit**: Goodbye.

Informationen über die Kultur der Inuit in Kanada lesen und verstehen;
einen Reim lesen ▶ S. 151

An e-mail for Colin

1 Read the e-mail. **2** Talk about the pictures.

E-mail

RE: Invitation
From: JohnMacDonald@email.com
To: ColinBaker@email.com

Dear Colin,
How are you? How's your trip? We're all fine.
My birthday is in three weeks. Please come
to my birthday party. It's at the farm.
All my friends and family will come, too.
Can you all come? Please let me know.

Your friend, John

John's birthday

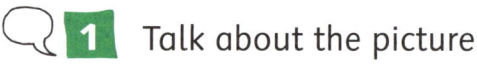
1 Talk about the picture.

budgie • cat • dog • horse • kangaroo • koala bear

Happy birthday, John!

Thank you, Colin.

Here's some orange juice.

I'm tired!

2 Talk to a partner.

I see something yellow.

Yes, it is. / No, it isn't.

Is it the bag?

3 Listen.

CD 2.03

Ein Bild beschreiben; Gegenstände nach Beschreibung erraten; einen Hörtext verstehen ▸ S. 157/158

Tom's daily routine

 1 Talk.

 2 Read about Tom's day.

I get up at 7 o'clock.

I have breakfast at 7.45 a.m.

School lessons start at 9 o'clock.

I have lunch at 12.30 p.m.

I finish school at 3 o'clock.

I help on the farm at 4 o'clock.

I play with my dog at 5.15 p.m.

I have dinner at 6 o'clock.

I go to bed at 8 o'clock.

| a.m. → in the morning |
| p.m. → in the afternoon |

 **3** Talk about your day.

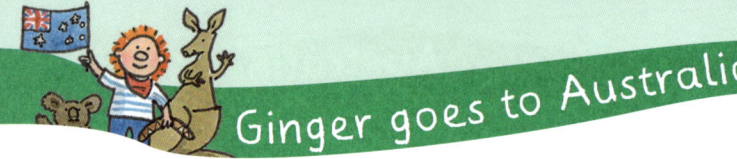

School at home

1 Talk. Read.

> book • glue • pen • pencil • pencil sharpener • rubber • ruler • scissors

Monday	Tuesday	Wednesday	Thursday	Friday
	Reading	Reading	On air private	Reading
Maths	Maths On air class	Maths	Maths	
Music		Drama	Science	Music On air class
Break				
English	English	English On air class		English
Lunch				
Science	Art/Craft	RE	Geography	
Break				
PE		PE	PE	PE

Have you got your ruler, Tom?

No, I haven't.

2 Talk to your partner.

Can I have your ruler, Sophie?

Sorry, I haven't got a ruler.

Can I have your ruler, Emma?

Yes, you can. Here you are.

Australian animals

 1 Read about the animals.

This is a wombat.
Wombats are small and strong.
They have small eyes.
Wombats are good swimmers.
They live in holes under the
ground.

This is an emu.
Emus are big birds,
but they can't fly.
They have a small head.
Emus have two long legs.
They can run very fast.
Emus live on the ground.

 **2** Read and talk about animals.

head ears eyes mouth nose legs feet toes tail		

big small long short	

can/can't	hop/jump run climb fly

... live
on the ground.
under the ground/in holes.
in trees.
in water.
in Australia.
in the mountains.
in caves.

Spotlight Landeskunde: School of the Air

 **1** Talk. Read.

School of the Air lesson
via radio

Can I help you with your presentation?

For School of the Air assemblies
pupils give presentations.
They sing a song, say a rhyme
or read a story.

It's your turn.

Pupils are having a break.
They are playing outside.

Can I have your homework, please?

Planes fly to farms in the Outback
once a week. The pilot collects and
drops off the homework.

 **2** Read the timetable. Talk about it.

	Monday	Tuesday	Wednesday	Thursday	Friday
9:00	Reading On air library	Reading	Reading	Reading	Reading
9:30	Maths	Maths On air class	Maths	Maths	Maths
10:30	Music	Art/Craft	Drama	Science	Music On air class
11:00			Break		
11:30	English	English	English On air class	English	English
12:30			Lunch		
1:30	Science	Art/Craft	RE	Geography	Drama
2:30			Break		
2:40	PE	PE	PE	PE	PE

On air private (30 minutes): Thursday

Informationen über die *School of the Air* im australischen Outback verstehen ▸ S. 173

A message for Dr Heal

1 Listen. Read the message for Dr Heal.

2.13

2 Talk about the pictures.

> Hi, Emily.
> It's me, Nombeko.
> Can you help me in the clinic?
> Please come to South Africa!
> Bye!

Ginger goes to South Africa

Welcome to Rivertown

CD 2.14

1 Listen. Where's the clinic, the school and Thabo's house?

Nurse Nombeko

Thabo

Grandma

Dr Heal

Eine Wegbeschreibung verstehen ▸ S. 179/180

The tortoise had a dream

 1 Listen. Talk about the pictures.

2.19

 2 Read the story.   **3** Act out.

1

There's a tree full of fruit and vegetables.

Haha, it was only a dream.

2

Do you know the tree?

Yes. The name is Omumbo-rombonga. But don't turn around!

3

What's the name of the tree? Amorom bing omerr? Oh no!

4

Be careful, there's a big rock.

5

What's the name of the tree? Bing bong bang? Oh no!

6

Be careful, there's a puddle of mud!

7

What's the name of the tree? Mimbim upo? Oh no!

8

Be careful, there's a river.

9

Omumbo-rombonga!

10

Eine Geschichte lesen und nachspielen ▶ S. 191/192

At the clinic

1 Talk about the pictures. Read the dialogue.

2 Act out.

Bilder beschreiben, einen Dialog lesen und nachspielen ▶ S. 187/188

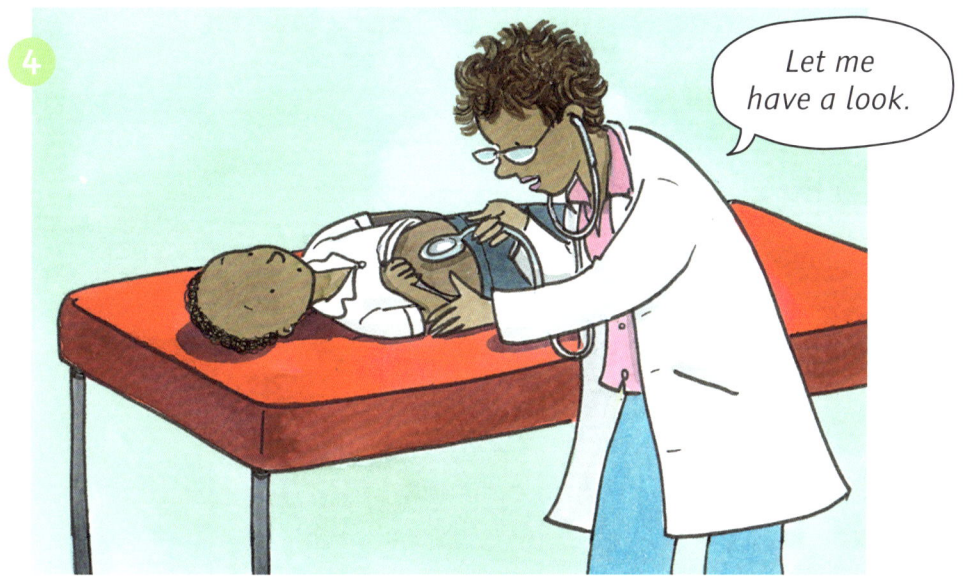

4

Let me have a look.

5

Here's some medicine for you.

6

You're welcome. Get well soon!

Thank you. Goodbye.

Spotlight Landeskunde: Animals in South Africa

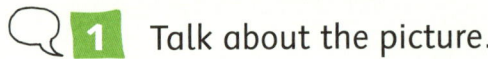

💬 **1** Talk about the picture.

💿🧑‍🏫 **2** Listen. Read the chant.

CD 2.21

In Africa, in Africa, there's a lot to see –
Lions, leopards and baboons in a tree.

Elephants, zebras and ostriches, too.
You meet them in nature, not in a zoo.

Penguins, giraffes and sharks in the sea –
Oh, what a wonderful place to be!

KRUGER
NATIONAL
PARK

OUDTSHOORN

ADDO ELEPHANT PARK

CAPE TOWN
CAPE POINT

MOSSEL BAY

Ein Bild beschreiben und über Tiere in Südafrika sprechen ▶ S. 195/196

An e-mail for Ravi

1 Talk about the pictures.   **2** Read the e-mail.

To:	Your visit
---	Mehta, Ravi
From:	Kumar, Hira

Dear Ravi,

We've got a new house!
It's big and very nice.
The children are happy in
the new house.
There's a small garden where
we can sit and drink tea.
The children like to play there.

Please come and visit us.

Love, Hira

Where's Ginger?

 **1** Talk about the picture. Where's Ginger?

 2 Listen. Act out the dialogue.

CD 2.25

> Is it a girl or a boy?
> Is she/he short or tall?
> What colour is her/his hair?
> What has she/he got on?

I've lost my friend.

Is it a boy or a girl?

Ein Bild beschreiben; einen Dialog nachspielen ▸ S.206

Manu and the snake

 1 Read the story. **2** Talk. What's missing in the pictures?

 3 Listen to the story.

CD 2.29

Grapefruits! Tasty grapefruits!

Are you scared?

The people and the cows liked
Manu's music.

Come and buy my skirts!

Are you scared?

Potatoes! Nice, new potatoes!

Are you scared?

Thank you, Manu!

Thank you very much.

Are you scared now, snake?

Manu put the snake into a basket.
Everybody was happy.

The snake danced to the music.

At the market

1 Talk about the pictures. Find 10 differences.

Bilder beschreiben und zehn Unterschiede finden ▸ S.213

Spotlight Landeskunde: People in India and their jobs

1 Talk about the pictures.

 2 Listen to the people.
CD 2.30

Amar

Rajesh

Kiran

Ranga

Sunita

Najuk

 3 Read the speech bubbles.

I'm an elephant trainer but I only work with one elephant. I'm a mahout.

I sing and dance in Bollywood films. They are often about love. I'm an actress.

I'm a taxi driver. But my taxi is not a car. It's a bike! I'm a rickshaw cyclist.

I want to be a cook. And you?

I work with computers. I make new programs and computer games. I'm a computer expert.

I work on a farm. We plant rice. I work 14 hours a day. I'm a paddy farmer.

I work in a clothing factory. I don't go to school. The money is for my family. I'm a factory worker.

Merry Christmas

I hear them

1 Talk about the pictures.

2 Sing the song and point to the pictures.

1 2 3 4

clop,
clop,
clop

I hear them, I hear them,
I hear them on the roof!
The reindeer are coming.
I hear each prancing hoof.
With a jingle, jingle bell
And a clop, clop, clop.
And a clatter, clatter, clatter
At the chimney top.
I hear them, I hear them,
I hear them on the roof!

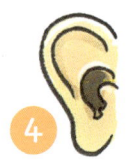

5

6 clatter,
clatter,
clatter

7

8

Bilder beschreiben; ein Lied singen und den Liedzeilen Abbildungen zuordnen ▶ S. 219

An Easter card

 1 Read. Make your Easter card.

You need: an envelope ✉   a card ▢   scissors ✂
glue 🫙   coloured pencils ✏

1
Fold the card.
Open the card.

2 
Draw a chicken.

3
3 cm
Colour the corner red.
Cut off the corner.
It's the beak.

4 
Glue the beak on the chicken.
Open the beak.
Fold the card and open it.

5 
Draw flowers and grass on your card.

6 
Write a message on your card.

Remember, remember

1 Talk about the pictures.

2 Listen to the rhyme. Read.

CD 2.36

Remember, remember

Remember, remember
the Fifth of November.
Gunpowder, treason and plot.
I see no reason
Why gunpowder treason
Should ever be forgot.

     Bilder beschreiben; einen Reim hören und lesen ▶ S. 223/224

Our trip around the world

1 Talk about the pictures.

2 Read.

London

In class 4 we went to London.
The Queen lives in Buckingham Palace.
There are big red buses in the streets.
Ginger is from London. He is our friend.

USA

We went to the USA.
New York is a very big city in the USA.
There were pirates on the beach in Los Angeles.
Debbie Jones is from the USA.
She is the radio operator on our ship.

Canada

We went to Canada.
There are a lot of mountains, rivers and lakes there.
There was a fish on Captain Storm's teepee.
Captain Storm is from Canada.
He is the captain on our ship.

South Africa

We went to South Africa.
There were bikes, chairs and tables on top of the buses.
Thabo had a tummy ache.
Dr Heal is from South Africa.
She is the doctor on our ship.

Australia

We went to Australia.
Australia is very big.
There are kangaroos hopping around.
Colin Baker is from Australia.
He is the cook on our ship.

India

We went to India.
There are lots of people and big markets there.
You can see cows in the street.
Ravi Metha is from India.
He is the mechanic on our ship.

Word list

A

a lot of viel/e
about über
again noch einmal
agree sich einig sein, zustimmen
all alle
all right in Ordnung
American football American Football
angry wütend
animal Tier
animal programme Tiersendung
April April
arm Arm
at bei, im, um
August August
aunt Tante
Australia Australien

B

back zurück
badminton Federball/ Badminton
badminton birdie Federball
bag Tasche
banana Banane
baseball Baseball
basket Korb
basketball Basketball
bathroom Badezimmer
be sein
beach Strand
beach ball Wasserball
beach towel Strandtuch
beak Schnabel
bear Bär
beaver Biber
because weil
bed Bett
bedroom Schlafzimmer
behind hinter
big groß
bike Fahrrad
bird Vogel
birdie Federball

birdcage Vogelkäfig
birthday Geburtstag
black schwarz
blond blond
blue blau
body Körper
book Buch
bonfire Lagerfeuer
boomerang Bumerang
boring langweilig
bottle Flasche
bowl Schale
box Kasten
boy Junge
breakfast Frühstück
brown braun
budgie Wellensittich
buffalo Büffel
bus Bus
bus stop Bushaltestelle
bush Strauch, Busch
busy beschäftigt
but aber
buy kaufen

C

camera Kamera, Foto- apparat
camping Zelten
can können
Canada Kanada
car Auto
card Karte
careful vorsichtig
carpet Teppich
carrot Mohrrübe
cartoon Zeichentrickfilm
cat Katze
CD player CD-Spieler
centimetre Zentimeter
chair Stuhl
cheese Käse
chicken Huhn
child Kind
children Kinder
city Stadt
class Klasse
clean saubermachen

clear klar, deutlich
clinic Klinik
clock Uhr
clothes Kleidung
coconut Kokosnuss
coin Münze
cold 1. kalt
2. Erkältung
collect sammeln
colour 1. Farbe
2. (aus)malen
come kommen
comic Comic(heft)
computer Computer
computer game Computerspiel
cookie Keks
correct richtig
cough Husten
coloured pencil Buntstift
count zählen
counter Spielstein
country Land
cow Kuh
crocodile Krokodil
crocus Krokus
cross überqueren
cut off abschneiden

D

dad Papa
daffodil Narzisse
dangerous gefährlich
day Tag
December Dezember
dice Würfel
dingo Dingo
dinner Abendessen
do machen
doctor Arzt/Ärztin
dog Hund
dollar Dollar
down herunter, unten
downstairs unten
draw zeichnen
dream Traum
drink trinken
duck Ente

E

eagle Adler
earache Ohrenschmerzen
Easter Ostern
Easter egg Osterei
eat essen
egg Ei
eighty achtzig
elephant Elefant
emu Emu
enjoy genießen
every jede/r/s
everybody alle
eye Auge

F

family Familie
famous berühmt
farm Bauernhof, Farm
fast schnell
father Vater
Father Christmas
  Weihnachtsmann
February Februar
feed füttern
feet Füße
fifty fünfzig
film Film
find finden
find out herausfinden
finish 1. Schluss
  2. aufhören, beenden
fireworks Feuerwerk
fish Fisch
flag Flagge
flower Blume
flute Flöte
fly fliegen
food Essen
foot Fuß
fold falten
football Fußball
for für
forget vergessen
forty vierzig
friend Freund/in
from von

fruit Obst
funny lustig

G

get werden, bekommen
get up aufstehen
giraffe Giraffe
girl Mädchen
give geben
glass Glas
glasses Brille
glue 1. Kleber 2. kleben
go gehen
gold Gold
good gut
goose Gans
grandpa Opa
grass Gras
Great Britain
  Großbritannien
green grün
ground Boden
guinea pig Meer-
  schweinchen
gunpowder Schießpulver
guy Kerl

H

hair Haar
half halb
hamburger Hamburger
hamster Hamster
happy glücklich
have got haben
has got hat
have haben
have a picnic picknicken
have lunch Mittag essen
head Kopf
headache Kopfschmerzen
help helfen
her ihr/e
here hier
his sein/e
hole Loch
holidays Ferien
homework Hausaufgaben

honey Honig
hope hoffen
hot heiß
house Haus
how wie
hundred hundert
hungry hungrig

I

idea Idee
in in
in front of vor
India Indien
information Information
instruction Anweisung
interesting interessant
into in (… hinein)
is ist
it es

J

January Januar
July Juli
June Juni
just nur

K

kangaroo Känguru
kill töten
kitchen Küche
kite Drachen
knee Knie
know wissen, kennen
koala Koala
kookaburra Kookaburra

L

lake See
left links
leg Bein
lesson Schulstunde,
  Lektion
let lassen
letter Brief
light Licht
like mögen
line 1. Reihe, Zeile 2. Linie

Word list

listen zuhören
live leben
living room Wohnzimmer
long lang
look schauen, sehen
look at sich etwas ansehen
loud laut
lunch Mittagessen

M

magazine Zeitschrift
maize Mais
make machen
man Mann
map Landkarte
March März
market Markt
market stand Marktstand
May Mai
meet treffen
medicine Medizin
melon Melone
message Nachricht
metre Meter
microphone Mikrofon
mobile phone Handy
money Geld
monkey Affe
moose Elch
mother Mutter
mountain Berg
mouse 1. Maus
   2. Computermaus
mouth Mund
much viel
mud Schlamm
mum Mama
music Musik
music show Musiksendung

N

name Name
narrator Erzähler
new neu
next Nächster, nächste
next to bei, neben
nice schön, nett

ninety neunzig
nose Nase
not nicht
November November
now jetzt
number 1. Nummer
   2. nummerieren
nurse Krankenschwester

O

o'clock Uhr
October Oktober
old alt
on an, auf
onion Zwiebel
only nur
on top oben, auf
ostrich Vogel Strauß
over über

P

page Seite
paper Papier
paper cup Pappbecher
paper towel Papierhand-
   tuch
past nach
peanut butter Erdnuss-
   butter
pen Füller
pencil Bleistift
pencil case Federmappe
pencil sharpener Bleistift-
   spitzer
penny Penny
people Menschen, Leute
pet Haustier
picnic Picknick
picture Bild
pineapple Ananas
pirate Pirat
play spielen
player Spieler
please bitte
plot Verschwörung
pocket knife Taschen-
   messer

police officer Polizist
poor arm
postcard Postkarte
pot Kanne, Topf
potato Kartoffel
pound Pfund
presentation Präsentation
press-up Liegestütz
programme Programm
puddle Pfütze
put setzen, stellen, legen

Q

quarter viertel
queen Königin
quiz show Ratesendung

R

rabbit Kaninchen
rat Ratte
read lesen
ready fertig
red rot
remember erinnern
repeat wiederholen
rhyme Reim
rice Reis
rich reich
right rechts
river Fluss
rock Stein
role-play Rollenspiel
room Zimmer
rubber Radiergummi
rubbish Abfall
rucksack Rucksack
ruler Lineal
run rennen

S

sad traurig
sand Sand
sandal Sandale
sandcastle Sandburg
say sagen
school Schule
scissors Schere

sea   Meer
seashell   Muschel
see   sehen
September   September
seventy   siebzig
shark   Hai
sheep   Schaf/e
shirt   Hemd
shoe   Schuh
short   1. kurz   2. klein
shoulder   Schulter
show   Aufführung
sister   Schwester
sixty   sechzig
skirt   Rock
sleep   schlafen
sleeping bag   Schlafsack
sleepy   schläfrig
small   klein
snow   Schnee
sock   Socke
some   etwas
something   etwas
soon   bald
sore throat   Halsschmerzen
sour cream   Sauerrahm
South Africa   Südafrika
speak   sprechen
sports programme   Sport-
   sendung
stamp   Briefmarke
stand   stehen
start   1. Beginn, Anfang
   2. beginnen, anfangen
stone   Stein
storeroom   Vorratskammer
straight   gerade
straight on   geradeaus
strong   stark
sun   Sonne
sunglasses   Sonnenbrille
sun hat   Sonnenhut
sweet potato   Süßkartoffel
swim   schwimmen
swimming
   costume   Badeanzug
swimming trunks   Bade-
   hose

T
table tennis   Tischtennis
take   nehmen
tall   groß
tea   Tee
teepee   Tipi
tent   Zelt
text message   SMS
there   dort
they   sie
thirty   dreißig
think   denken
throw   werfen
tick   abhaken
ticket   Fahrschein
ticket machine
   Fahrkartenautomat
tired   müde
to   nach, zu
toe   Zeh
toilet   Toilette
top   oben
torch   Taschenlampe
tortoise   Schildkröte
touch   berühren
town   Stadt
track   Spur
train   Zug
travel   reisen
treason   Verrat
treasure chest   Schatzkiste
tree   Baum
trousers   Hose
tulip   Tulpe
tummy   Bauch
tummy ache   Bauchweh
turn   abbiegen, umdrehen
turn around   umdrehen,
   wenden
twenty-one   einund-
   zwanzig
twin   Zwilling

U
uncle   Onkel
under   unter
underground   unter der
   Erde

underline   unterstreichen
up   oben, auf, herauf
upstairs   oben
USA   Vereinigte Staaten
   von Amerika

V
vegetable   Gemüse
very   sehr
volleyball   Volleyball

W
walk   gehen
want   wollen
watch   1. Armbanduhr
   2. zusehen, zuschauen
water   Wasser
water bottle   Wasser-
   flasche
we   wir
wear   anhaben, tragen
well   gesund, gut
what   was
where   wo
white   weiß
who   wer
why   warum
with   mit
wolf   Wolf
wombat   Wombat
word   Wort
world   Welt
write   schreiben
wrong   falsch

Y
yellow   gelb
Yuck!   Igitt!